THORESBY HALL

Nottinghamshire

Once the seat of the Pierrepont family and home of the Countess Manvers

AN HISTORIC HOTEL

Thoresby is a magnificent Victorian Grade I listed hall which has been fully restored to its former glory. It was built for the 3rd Earl Manvers by the renowned architect of the day, Anthony Salvin, and has now been transformed into the glorious country hotel you see today.

This book is a celebration of Thoresby Hall; its history and former treasures, and the families whose home it once was.

Opposite left:
The Arms of
the late Earl Manvers

Detail from an 18th
century Urn Clock

CONTENTS

THORESBY & THE PIERREPONTS 4

A TOUR OF THE HALL 8

THE ENTRANCE 9

THE GREAT HALL 10

VICTORIA SUITE 14

THE BALCONY GALLERY 17

THE BLUE DRAWING ROOM 18

THE LIBRARY 20

THE SMALL DRAWING ROOM 24

THE STATE DINING ROOM 26

THE GARDENS AND PARK 29

ROBIN HOOD AND SHERWOOD FOREST 32

THORESBY HALL TODAY 35

ALL WITHIN AN HOUR'S DRIVE 36

Thoresby House by Tillemans 1725

PIE REPONE TE

THORESBY AND THE PIERREPONTS

THROUGH the centuries the family name has been spelt in nine different ways and for the sake of clarity the modern version has been used throughout.

The Pierreponts are of Norman extraction. **ROBERT DE PIERREPONT**, the first of whom any mention is found, was a companion of **WILLIAM THE CONQUEROR** and came over to England with him at the Conquest. Robert first held lands in Sussex and was succeeded by his son **WILLIAM**, who in turn was succeeded by **HUGH DE PIERREPONT**. His

son, **WILLIAM**, acquired the Lordship of Haliwell in Lancashire and married Beatrix, only daughter of William, Baron Warren of Norfolk. Their elder son, who succeeded, fought at the battle of Lewes and was taken prisoner with Henry III and his grandson **HENRY DE PIERREPONT** was the first member of the family to settle at Holme which he acquired through his marriage with **ANNORA DE MANVERS** in **1314**. The elder son of this marriage, **ROBERT, BECAME GOVERNOR OF NEWARK CASTLE**. He was summoned to Parliament as a Baron but died before he took his seat. His elder son was succeeded for four generations by elder sons, all of whom were buried at Holme Pierrepont. **HENRY DE PIERREPONT** won distinction under Edward IV and was knighted for his services against the Lancastrians. At the dissolution of the monasteries by **HENRY VIII**, his son and heir, George, purchased several large estates and manors, became staunchly loyal to the Protestant succession and received the honour of knighthood in the first year of the reign of Edward VI. He died early in Elizabeth's reign, being at the time possessed of Holme Pierrepont, near Nottingham, besides nine other manors. **ROBERT**, grandson of George and an ardent cavalier, married Frances, daughter of **SIR WILLIAM CAVENDISH** and **BESS OF HARDWICK**. In the service of Charles I he acquitted himself with boldness and success and was created **BARON PIERREPONT, VISCOUNT NEWARK** and, in 1628, **EARL OF KINGSTON**. When Lieutenant-General of the Royalist forces and professing himself desirous of peace, but fully resolved not to act on either side, he swore: "*When I take arms with the King against Parliament, or with Parliament against the King, let a cannon-ball divide me between them*", which, writes a chronicler of the day, "*God was pleased to bring to pass a few months after - for he, going to Gainsborough, and there taking up arms for the King was surprised by Lord Willoughby, and after a handsome defence of himself, yielded and was put prisoner into a pinnace and sent down the river to Hull. When my Lord Newcastle's army, marching along the shore, shot at the pinnace, my Lord Kingston being in danger went up on deck to show himself and to prevail with them to forbear shooting, but as soon as he appeared a cannon-ball flew from the King's army and divided him in the middle, being then in the Parliament's pinnace, who perished according to his own unhappy imprecation*". The first Earl's portrait hung in the Great Hall at Thoresby. The Royalist version of this melancholy affair is that the attack on the pinnace was an attempt by the King's army to rescue the Earl. The stormy years that followed saw his sons ranged on opposite sides. **HENRY, THE 2ND EARL**, remained loyal to the Stuarts, the younger, **WILLIAM**, joined the Parliamentary party and became an intimate and highly respected adviser to **CROMWELL**.

Evelyn 5th Earl, who became 1st Duke of Kingston

HENRY, who was well-versed in both the law and medicine (his bust is in the Royal College of Physicians to whom he left his large medical library), was created Marquess of Dorchester in 1643 which title became extinct at his death in 1680. Three grand-nephews successively inherited the earldom and the third, **EVELYN, 5TH EARL**, received a renewal of the extinct Marquessate in 1706 and, in 1715, the Dukedom of Kingston-upon-Hull. Besides other honours which were bestowed upon him by the Crown, he was three times appointed one of the lords justices when the King went to Hanover. He married

first, **MARY, DAUGHTER OF WILLIAM FEILDING, EARL OF DENBIGH** and later **LADY ISABELLA BENTINCK, SISTER OF HENRY, DUKE OF PORTLAND. EVELYN PIERREPONT, 2ND DUKE OF KINGSTON**, succeeded to the title at the age of fifteen. He was a nephew of **LADY MARY WORTLEY MONTAGU** who said of him shortly after his succession: *"he has hitherto had so ill an education, 'tis hard to make any judgment of him; he has his spirit, but I fear will never have his father's sense but, as young gentlemen go, 'tis possible he may make a good figure amongst them"*. In **1771** he was appointed a Lord of the Bedchamber. He is described by **WALPOLE** as being *"possessed of the greatest beauty and the finest person in England"*. The Duke's purported marriage to **MISS ELIZABETH CHUDLEIGH** of Ashton, County Devon, caused the sensation of the century. Elizabeth Chudleigh when attending Winchester Races met there the **HON. AUGUSTUS JOHN HERVEY** who was a lieutenant in the Navy. They fell violently in love and Hervey obtained short leave of absence when they were married privately at Lainston Church on the evening of 4th August, **1744**, the ceremony being performed by the incumbent, the Rev. Thomas Amis. The reason for secrecy was that, owing to the young couple's lack of means, the bride had decided so long as her husband was on foreign service to retain her post of Maid of Honour to **AUGUSTA**, consort of Frederick, Prince of Wales, at a salary of £400 a year, which as a married woman she could not have done. That there then began a liaison between Elizabeth and the Duke of Kingston is beyond doubt and it began not later than **1750**. When she was not in waiting she and the Duke paid occasional visits to Thoresby and the Duke later purchased a plot of ground at Knightsbridge upon which he erected a great mansion, which was known as Kingston House. This Elizabeth furnished in her own style. It was just at this time that a blow fell upon her. To her surprise she received a

Elizabeth Chudleigh, Countess of Bristol, who bigamously married the 2nd Duke of Kingston

~ 'sensation of the century'

communication from her husband to the effect that he proposed to take proceedings for divorce. This communication was in a way welcome to Elizabeth for there was little doubt that if she were free the Duke of Kingston would marry her. On the other hand, she was particularly anxious that she should not appear as the guilty party. Obviously, there could be no divorce if there had been no marriage and, wishing to destroy the proofs of her marriage, she went one day to the church at Lainston, and bribed the clerk to let her abstract the register on which her marriage was recorded. The Consistory Court of London which followed gave judgment in favour of Elizabeth and pronounced her to be free of all matrimonial contracts or espousals. Elizabeth, being thus pronounced a spinster, was now able to wed her lover, "*who*", wrote Horace Walpole at the time, "*was not reluctant to make an honest woman of his mistress*". On her "*marriage*" Elizabeth ceased to be a Lady-in-Waiting to the Princess Dowager and they continued to reside at Thoresby, at the Duke's estate at Bath, and at Kingston House, Knightsbridge. The Duke died in 1773 at the age of 61 after four years of marriage.

The "Duchess" whose legal husband, HERVEY, had succeeded to the earldom of Bristol, was accused of bigamy and, as she was legally Countess of Bristol, was tried and found guilty by the House of Lords. She spent the rest of her life abroad. CHARLES MEDOWS, son of LADY FRANCES MEDOWS, the Duke's elder sister, now succeeded to the unencumbered estates of his uncle the 2nd and last Duke of Kingston having disposed of the claims of the "Duchess", and assumed the surname and arms of Pierrepont. He was M.P. for Nottinghamshire from 1778-96 and was created Baron Pierrepont and Viscount Newark in 1796 and Earl Manvers in 1806. On his death in 1816 he was succeeded by his son CHARLES HERBERT who married MARY LAETITIA, daughter of Anthony Hardolph Eyre of Grove, Nottingham. Sydney William Herbert succeeded his father as 3rd Earl in 1860, and represented South Nottingham in the House of Commons from 1852 until his succession to the Peerage eight years later. He married GEORGINE JANE ELIZABETH FANNY DE FRANQUETOT, daughter of GUSTAVE, DUC DE COIGNY.

The 5th and last Earl Manvers died in 1955 leaving a widow and an only daughter, LADY ROZELLE RAYNES.

The Countess Manvers

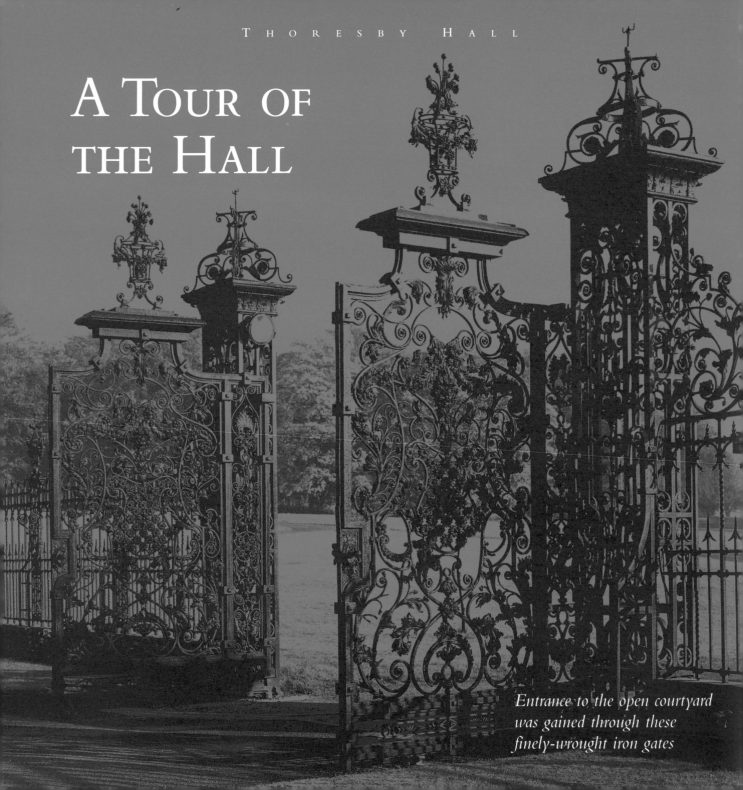

A TOUR OF THE HALL

*Entrance to the open courtyard
was gained through these
finely-wrought iron gates*

THE ENTRANCE

THORESBY HALL is perhaps unique in that it is essentially a product of the Victorian age. It has been a continuously lived-in home and its Victorian character was preserved to a remarkable degree. The square, gabled tower, numerous turrets and balustrades, dominate the skyline. The main south and east fronts, are 182 and 180 feet in length respectively. Entrance to the open courtyard was gained by passing through the finely-wrought iron main gates.

The entrance was on the east under a central tower in the style of Burghley House in Stamford; the windows left and right are symmetrical, but the irregularity which Victorian designers cherished has made the corner motifs conspicuously different.

The Entrance Hall as it was in 1978

Left: Detail of the finely-wrought iron gates

THE GREAT HALL

At the top of the stairs, the Sherwood oak double doors open into the Great Hall.

The Great Hall painted by Lady Manvers, an artist of considerable attainment

The panelling is of white and red oak from Sherwood Forest. The south side is dominated by an elaborate stone fireplace embellished with the Pierrepont coat-of-arms.

Magnificently proportioned, it is 64 feet long, 31 feet across and 50 feet in height, rising through three storeys to an open hammerbeam roof.

*The Great Hall
in 1978*

A family group painted by Vanderbank

Photographs courtesy of the Newark Advertiser

In the Spring of 1957, Thoresby Hall opened its
doors to the general public for the first time.
The starlet Sabrina was employed at the press launch
to lend glamour to the event in the guise of
Maid Marian. In one picture (above), she posed on
the Grand Staircase and in another she cuddles up
to 'Robin Hood'; a statue by Tussaud-Birt,
a grandson of Madame Tussaud. The statue
which stood in the centre of the courtyard is now
to be seen in the Stables Gallery.

The Victoria Suite has been beautifully renovated,
to create a **Royale Room**

14

VICTORIA SUITE

At the west end of the Hall is the Grand Staircase with its large equestrian portrait of Charles I, so well placed that the monarch appears to be on the point of riding down the staircase into the Hall. Turning left and continuing up the staircase was the Gold Bedroom, the first of the bedrooms which were furnished in keeping with the period of the house; the furniture, chiefly of amboyna wood, being specially constructed for Thoresby. The feature of the period was, of course, the tendency to clutter every room with an abundance of ornaments and trinkets, but the bedrooms struck a pleasant balance between the preservation of their Victorian character and the minimum of ornamentation. In the next room there were the complicated but colourful, robes of a peer and peeress worn by the late Earl Manvers and the last Countess at the Coronation of H M Queen Elizabeth II.

Beyond was the Victoria Room in which numerous pieces of furniture, all of the period of William and Mary, were particularly admired for the simplicity of their design. Although the Victoria Room was much less magnificent than some of the suites of the period, it conformed to a certain simplicity which it is known was the taste of Queen Victoria. The wallpaper was specially

A room from the Victoria Suite in 1978

designed for the room and was hand-painted on the premises by a well known specialist in interior decoration, Mr. Guy Marson. It was typical of the period of the house, and the theme was based on the Pierrepont crest. Although modern lighting was used throughout Thoresby, the Victoria Room, as well as other rooms, contained specimens of the original oil lamps in use when the house was first occupied. The history of lighting at Thoresby ran from oil lamps, via gas from a small gasworks in the grounds, and an electric generating plant in the out-buildings to the present mains supply. The chimneypiece was by John de Val and was brought from the second house at Thoresby when it was demolished. The large mirror-glass over it was of a style much in vogue at the time and was typical of many others hanging in the other rooms of Thoresby Hall. Although only the State Bedrooms were open to the public, there was a very large number of bedrooms in the house, showing that there would have been many guests staying for house parties, shoots and the like, and this draws attention to the staff. Records show that when the house was first lived in there were 46 indoor servants, and over 50 outdoor servants - gardeners and grooms. Although no records of wages are available for 1871 when the house was first staffed, those paid in the days of the First World War may be of interest for comparison: the butler - £85 a year, the housekeeper -£50, the fifth houseman - £14, and the second groom - £28. At that time it was necessary to have a licence for each male servant and 24 licences were applied for in the year 1917. Other interesting items included an allowance of two shillings a week to the maid-servants for beer, but this allowance was merged into increased wages in 1919. Many of the tenants paid a shilling a week into a clothing club run by the then Countess Manvers, as well as contributing to the Thoresby Nursing Association for the services of the District Nurse.

The estate accounts for the year 1871 showed payments which appear unrealistic, the rates on the Hall were only £19. 13. 9d. per half year, but 'House Duty' of £18. 15. 0d. was payable. All transport was by horse-drawn vehicles and the wages of the grooms and the feeding stuffs, etc., cost £1261.10. 2½d., which translated would mean an expenditure today of at least £150,000 a year.

Marie-Louise Rooseveldt Bourke, grandmother to Lady Manvers in the Victoria Room

16

THE BALCONY GALLERY

Below left and right: Pencil portraits by Lady Manvers

On emerging from the bedrooms the visitor would enter the Balcony Gallery on the walls of which hung a collection of Lady Manvers' earlier works, some of which had been exhibited in London and Paris. Countess Manvers was a member of the Society of Women Artists and her pictures had been hung in the Royal Academy and in the Salon in Paris. At one end of the Gallery hung portraits of the Ist Earl of Kingston and the notorious 'Duchess' of Kingston, of whom more later, and portraits of other members of the Pierrepont family were hung in the Gallery. These are occasionally on display in the Stables Gallery.

The Blue Room has been beautifully renovated to create the á la carte restaurant, specialising in contemporary British and European cuisine -

the perfect place to relax.

THE BLUE
DRAWING ROOM

Entrance to the Blue Drawing Room was gained by passing through the door at the south-west corner of the Great Hall and it took its name from the blue silk damask with which the walls were covered; the woodwork is of walnut and maple. The marble chimneypieces represented the four seasons. The panels on the walls were French rococo and showed a style of decoration which was popular throughout the greater part of Europe during the first half of the 18th century and which enjoyed a renewed vogue at the time the house was built.

The 3rd Earl Manvers and his Countess, born Georgine Jane Elizabeth Fanny de Franquetot, daughter of Gustave, Duc de Coigny

THE LIBRARY

The woodwork in the Library is light and dark oak. The Library occupies the centre of the south front suite and the books numbered some five thousand, the emphasis being largely on books of history and exploration. Many of the earlier books owned by the Pierrepont family were destroyed when the first Thoresby Hall was burnt, and therefore the contents of the previous Library dated from the mid-18th century. Thoresby was the remaining portion of the original Pierrepont estates, and these were originally

The Library from 1978

spread over many parts of England, the original documents preserved included the plans and schedules of lands now sold, but many of the original documents have been deposited with Nottingham University to assist in research into county history.

The view from the Library windows is particularly fine and also of interest as you look towards the original Thoresby, the first two houses having been on a site between the present cricket ground and the lake, and the foundations of the second house may still be seen. There has also been change in the landscape, the sloping ground between the trees on the far side of the lake was originally a cascade which was a major feature visible from the first house, and the area around the foundations shows signs of the original landscaping and is still known as the 'Pleasure Grounds'. A feature of Thoresby has always been the herd of deer, and although these are very shy they may sometimes be seen amongst the trees of this area. Thoresby Park extends to approximately 3000 acres within the boundaries of the A614 and A616 roads and the junction with the adjoining National Trust property of Clumber Park. Thoresby and Clumber together with the adjoining Welbeck properties form the area known as 'The Dukeries' originally in the ownership of the Dukes of Kingston (Thoresby), the Dukes of Newcastle (Clumber) and the Dukes of Portland (Welbeck) from the 17th century onwards. The present owners are Lady Rozelle Raynes, the only daughter of the late Lord Manvers and the Trustees of the Thoresby Settlement, The National Trust and the trustees of the late Duke of Portland.

In spite of the development of the Park, it has not lost its charm as part of Sherwood Forest, the beauty of its woods and fields being most enjoyable in spring and early autumn with the varied colouring of the many varieties of trees and shrubs, although the summer has a beauty all its own with rhododendrons and azaleas.

The elaborately carved fireplace, depicting the Major Oak at Edwinstowe is supported by statues of Robin Hood and Little John and was carried out over three years by a local craftsman from Mansfield.

The Small Drawing Room in 1978

THE SMALL DRAWING ROOM

On leaving the Library, you entered the Small Drawing Room, the particularly beautiful floor being of maple inlaid with satinwood.

Grace Pierrepont,
Lady of the Bedchamber
to Queen Anne

Below: Lady Mary
Grant, daughter of the
4th Earl Manvers

THE STATE DINING ROOM

EVELYN 1st Duke of Kingston, CHARLES 2nd Earl of Burlington and LORD BERKELEY of Stratton by Michael Dahl

The State Dining Room is of noble proportions, and was given over to the exhibition of interesting collections which were changed from time to time. The paintings in the room were dominated by portraits of the Emperor Napoleon III and the Empress Eugenie at St. Cloud by Boutibonne on the south wall.

The table, depicted, was set for a small dinner party with typical specimens of family and china and glass as a small reminder of the days when entertaining was on much more lavish a scale than is now possible. This is also reflected in the records which show that when the house was first occupied there were 46 indoor servants as compared with the mere handful of retainers who now perform miracles of cleanliness and tidiness. Although no records of wages in 1871 are available, those paid in the days of the first World War may be of interest for comparison: the butler £85 a year, the Housekeeper - £50, the Houseman - £14 and the 2nd Groom - £28. At that time it was necessary to have a licence for each male servant and 24 licences were applied for in the year 1917.

The State Dining Room pictured in 1978

The State Dining Room was dominated by two impressive portraits of the Empress Eugenie at St. Cloud, and the Emperor Napoleon III by Boutibonne

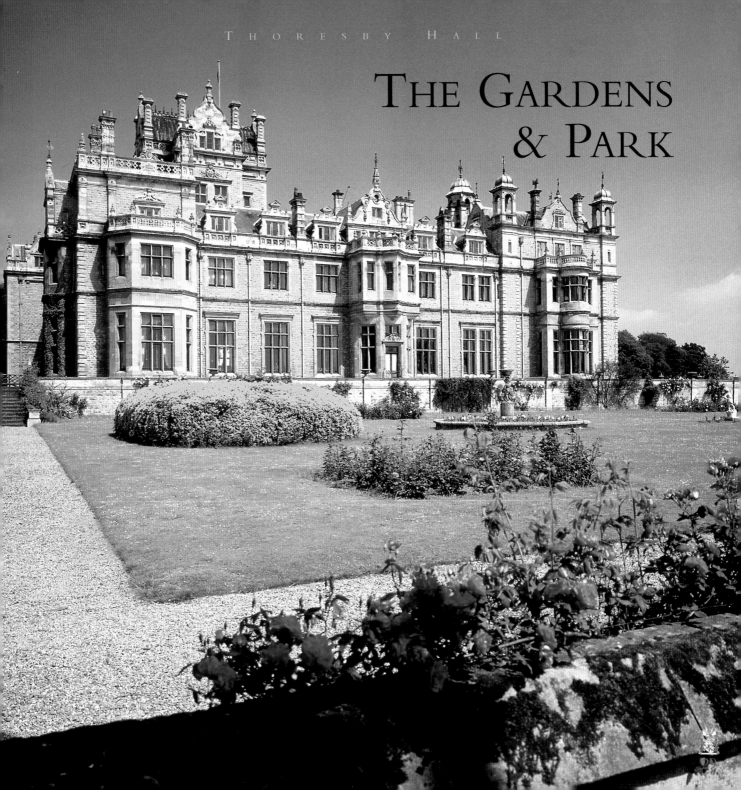

The Gardens & Park

The grounds immediately surrounding the Hall extend to some fifty acres. The remaining portions of the Thoresby Estate within North Nottinghamshire extend to over 12,000 acres, and even this is only a fraction of the area owned by the earlier members of the Pierrepont family, not only locally but in Somerset and elsewhere.

Left:
The South Front Gardens

Until the Second World War Thoresby Park was, as its name indicated, the parkland of Thoresby Hall, but with the need for food and timber production a rapid change came upon the scene after 1939. The Hall was requisitioned and in the occupation of the Military for the duration of the war, part of the parklands was taken over by the County War Agricultural Executive and given over to the production of food crops and major fellings of timber took place during the war years.

The celebrated designer of Thoresby Hall, Anthony Salvin, was the doyen of Victorian revivalist architecture, and his work can be seen at many 'stately homes', such as Alnwick Castle in Northumberland and Windsor Castle. Although his design and decorative stonework at Thoresby reminds one of Elizabethan mansions such as Burghley House, Stamford and Wollaton Hall near Nottingham, this gazebo dates from the 1860s.

Robin Hood & Sherwood Forest

Thoresby is closely associated with Sherwood Forest and its legends of Robin Hood, the hero who, according to tradition, roamed with his trusty band through these forest glades with their masses of bracken, and broom, heather and gorse, and recesses in sturdy old oaks, and whose name and fame have been handed down through seven long centuries, and who has been claimed by other areas and towns.

A 16th century manuscript in the British Museum tells us that Robin Hood was born at Loxley in Yorkshire, but there is some doubt about this. The date of his birth is also uncertain, but he is thought to have been born in the reign of Henry II about the year 1160 and to have lived for 87 years, though most of what we know is folklore.

Figures of Little John and Robin Hood from the elaborate chimneypiece in the Library. This stunning piece of work took three years to complete and was carved by Richard John Tuddesbury of Edwinstowe, the site of the carving's centrepiece, the Major Oak.

Photograph here and top right:
Nottinghamshire County Council

The Major Oak
~ legend has it that the famous outlaw used this tree as his hideout. Today this ancient tree is a great tourist attraction for visitors from around the world.

Adopting a life in the woods he made his home in Sherwood Forest where he was joined by Little John, Will Scarlet, Maid Marian and Friar Tuck and in course of time his company of outlaws consisted of a hundred of the most expert archers who were a match for more than four times their number. Chivalrous to women, the protector of the widow and fatherless, the friend of the needy and oppressed, he robbed the rich and powerful to relieve the poor and distressed. The ballads tell of many pranks he played on the Sheriff of Nottingham who, as the representative of law and order, was supposed to put a stop to his activities.

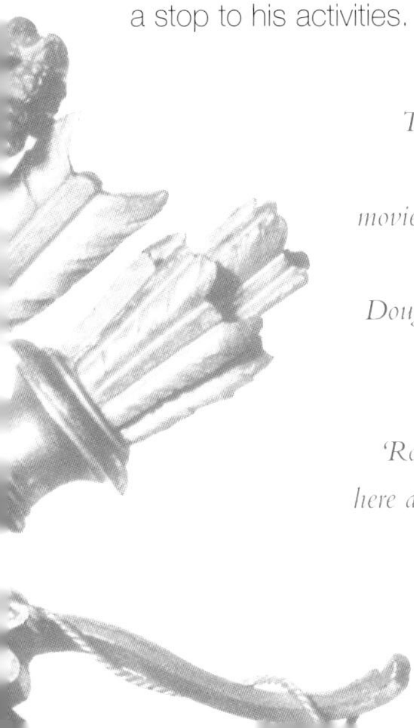

The story of Robin Hood has fuelled the imagination of moviemakers throughout the history of cinema, from films featuring Douglas Fairbanks to Kevin Costner and Sean Connery. Arguably the greatest and possibly most famous 'Robin' was **Errol Flynn**, *seen here at his most dashing in the 1938 picture 'The Adventures of Robin Hood'.*

Photograph courtesy of Mirror Syndication International

33

THORESBY HALL TODAY

Not only is Thoresby Hall a listed house, but so too are its GARDENS. There are few more enjoyable ways of passing the time than strolling around these magnificent grounds, playing BOWLS on the green, or trying your hand at ARCHERY, CROQUET or TENNIS. There is also a GOLF PRACTICE net and CYCLE HIRE facility.

The inside of the hall has been carefully and sensitively restored so don't leave without looking around THE GREAT HALL, THE BLUE ROOM, THE BILLIARD AND ANTE ROOM.

In addition to the original part of the hall, you'll find every modern facility including a purpose-built CABARET VENUE featuring nightly entertainment, RESTAURANT, À LA CARTE RESTAURANT, COFFEE SHOP, LOUNGES, BARS, SHOP and CONFERENCE FACILITIES. Aromatherapy massage, facials and a solarium are available at our HEALTH AND BEAUTY FACILITY. And for the energetic, there is a superb INDOOR SWIMMING POOL AND SPA complete with SAUNA and STEAM ROOM as well as a FITNESS STUDIO with a thriving LEISURE CLUB available to local residents. After all this pleasure, why not relax with a stroll in the beautiful Hall Grounds or enjoy a longer walk around the Estate.

All within an hour's drive...

This part of the country has its own unique history and offers lots to see and do. It would be impossible to visit the area without exploring the picturesque and romantic Sherwood Forest which sits right on the Hotel's doorstep.

Close by is the delightful historic parkland of Clumber Park, the only working watermill in Nottinghamshire at Ollerton and, at Rufford Country Park, the remains of a 12th century Cistercian Abbey and a contemporary Craft and Ceramics Centre. Slightly further afield is Mr Straw's house in Worksop which has been left untouched since the 1920s and 30s and is a fascinating piece of social history. Lord Byron's ancestral home, Newstead Abbey is just south of Mansfield and the beautiful Georgian town of Southwell and its famous Minster also within easy reach. At Eastwood you can visit D. H. Lawrence's Birthplace Museum. And Nottingham and Lincoln are but a short drive away.

Photographs courtesy of
Nottinghamshire County Council